Test Your Business English

Hotel and Catering

Alison Pohl

Series Editor: Nick Brieger

PENGUIN BOOKS

PENGUIN BOOKS

Published by the Penguin Group
Penguin Books Ltd, 27 Wrights Lane, London W8 5TZ England
Penguin Books USA Inc., 375 Hudson Street, New York, New York 10014, USA
Penguin Books Australia Ltd, Ringwood, Victoria, Australia
Penguin Books Canada Ltd, 10 Alcorn Avenue, Toronto, Ontario, Canada M4V 3B2
Penguin Books (NZ) Ltd, 182–190 Wairau Road, Auckland 10, New Zealand

Penguin Books Ltd, Registered Offices: Harmondsworth, Middlesex, England

Published by Penguin Books 1996
10 9 8 7 6 5 4 3 2 1

Printed in England by Clays Ltd, St Ives plc
Set in 9.25/13.5pt Monophoto Times

INTRODUCTION

Language knowledge and communication skills are the basic tools for developing competence in a foreign language. Vocabulary, together with a command of grammar and pronunciation, are the main components of language knowledge.

This series aims to develop the vocabulary required by professionals and pre-service students. The materials provide clear and simple test materials of around 500 key concepts and terms in various professional areas. Each book is devoted to one professional area, divided into eight sections. Each section, focusing on one topic area, tests the knowledge of both concepts and terms. The materials can be used as part of a language course for specialists or as a handy reference for self-study.

For the first books, we have chosen areas which are of significant current interest in the business world. Each has been written by an author with considerable practical experience in the field and we hope that the series will prove a valuable aid to users.

ABOUT THIS BOOK

Test Your Business English: Hotel and Catering is for people working in the hotel and catering industry who are not native speakers of English. It aims to help them:
• check their knowledge of basic concepts and key terms (words and expressions) used in their industry
• see how these terms are used so that they can use them effectively and successfully themselves.

The book will also be a useful source of information for trainers who need to run courses for hotel and catering personnel.

The material has been designed for self-study or classroom use by learners at intermediate level or above.

Organization of the material
The book is divided into eight sections and each section deals with an important part of the hotel and catering industry. In this way it is organized more like a textbook than a test book, with individual sections devoted to individual areas. We have chosen to do this so that, if they wish, learners can work through each section and see how terms group together. We believe this will help learners develop their range of expression in a structured and systematic way.

After the tests, there is:
• a complete answer key
• an appendix of American-English terms
• a full A–Z word list.

Using the material
The Contents page shows the eight main areas covered. Learners can either work through the book from the beginning or select sections according to their interests or needs. After each test, learners should check their answers. While working on a test, learners may come across unknown or unfamiliar words. This is an opportunity for them to check their understanding and extend their knowledge. So, a good dictionary of general English as well as a more specialist dictionary will be useful companions to this volume. In this way, the material in this book can be used both for testing and for teaching.

Selection of the terms
The terms are directly relevant to the work of people working in hotel and catering. Very general terms are not included, nor are very technical ones. The language model is predominantly British English.

CONTENTS

1 Lost property

These items have been left behind by customers. Write the number of each item next to the correct word or words. (See example):

binoculars	11
cap	......
carrier bag	......
compact	......
doll	......
glasses	......
glove	......
keys	......
lipstick	......
pocket diary	......
purse	......
ski stick	......
tie	......
toilet bag	......
umbrella	......

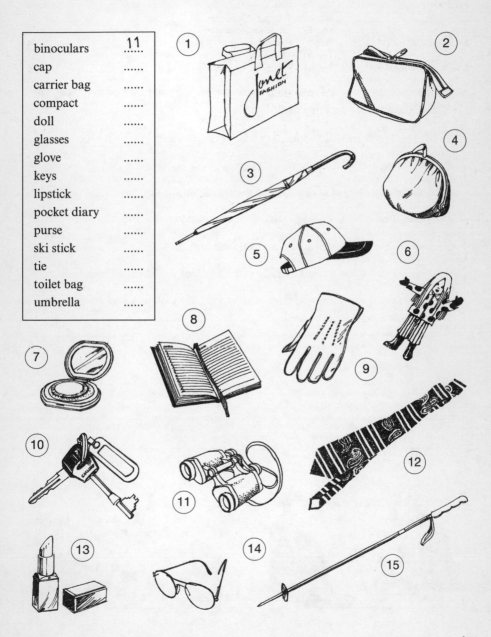

2 Guest relations

What does the receptionist say to the hotel guests? Write the letter of each phrase in the speech bubble of the correct picture. (See example):

a) 'Could you spell that, please?'

b) 'Good evening, sir. May I help you?'

c) 'I'm afraid your room isn't quite ready yet. Would you mind taking a seat in the lounge for a few minutes?'

d) 'I'm sorry you've had to wait, madam. How can I help you?'

e) 'Of course, sir. I'll call you when it comes.'

f) 'I'm terribly sorry that you're not happy with your room.'

g) 'Could I possibly ask you to park your car round the back?'

h) 'One moment, please madam, and I'll work out the total.'

i) 'Can I suggest you try our evening entertainment. It's always very popular.'

j) 'I'm so glad you've enjoyed your stay with us. We look forward to welcoming you back again in the future.'

3 Reception

Choose the word which best completes each sentence.

1 Guests entering the hotel will find the reception desk in the ....
   a) scullery   b) foyer   c) back office   d) corridor

2 One of the jobs of a receptionist is to .... complaints.
   a) manage   b) deal with   c) organize   d) regret

3 People who use the same hotel on several occasions are called ....
   a) normals   b) returners   c) regulars   d) usuals

4 Customers with valuable items should use the .... provision.
   a) safe deposit   b) secure   c) savings   d) lock up

5 The people who use a particular hotel are known as the ....
   a) guest list   b) long stays   c) clientele   d) usuals

6 When guests arrive the receptionist usually asks them to sign the ....
   a) register   b) bookings form   c) ledger   d) guest bill

7 Each day the .... list shows the names of the guests expected.
   a) stop-go   b) records   c) arrivals   d) room

8 If guests lose their room keys, a member of staff can open their room door with
   a .... key.
   a) main   b) passage   c) pass   d) card

9 Messages for guests who are out should be placed in the appropriate ....
   at reception.
   a) pigeon hole   b) key hole   c) bird box   d) key hook

10 Hotels may manage to fill vacant rooms with .... bookings.
   a) opportunity   b) chance   c) early   d) provisional

11 People who have booked but don't arrive are known as ....
   a) delays   b) no comers   c) failures   d) no shows

12 In order to be successful, a hotel must try to maximize room ....
   a) availability   b) turnover   c) status   d) occupancy

4 Reservations

The following extracts are from two different letters, a letter making a reservation and a letter of confirmation, but they have got mixed up. Put them in the right order to produce two correct letters.

1
> Yours faithfully
> Susan Peacock
> Secretary

2
> I look forward to receiving your confirmation.

3
> I would like to reserve four single rooms from 19th to 24th November 19– for four of our managers.

4
> We look forward to receiving our guests.

5
> Dear Sir/Madam

6
> Thank you for your letter of 16th September 19–. We are very pleased that you have chosen to use our hotel for your four managers who will be in Anyton from 19th to 24th November 19–.

7
> The rooms should be booked in the names of John Brown, Mary Black, Bill Franks and Ann Jones.

8
> Could you please inform me of your rates and whether you offer discounts for company bookings.

9
> I would like to confirm your reservation for four single rooms for these dates. We are happy to be able to offer you our corporate rates, which you will find in the enclosed leaflet.

10
> Yours sincerely
> Peter Black
> Reservations Clerk

11
> Dear Ms Peacock

letter of reservation

☐ ☐ ☐ ☐ ☐ ☐

letter of confirmation

☐ ☐ ☐ ☐ ☐

5

5 Word building 1

The word in capitals at the end of each sentence can be used to form a word that fits suitably in the blank space. (See example):

Customers usually make a phone call or send a
fax to make a ....*reservation*.................... .   RESERVE

1 I'm not sure of the exact dates yet so I'd like to make a
   ...\.................................... booking for the 24th to 28th.   PROVISION

2 They made a booking for twenty people but it isn't a
   .... booking yet.   CONFIRMATION

3 There are more guests than rooms. I'm afraid the hotel is
   ....   BOOKING

4 I'm sorry, but there is no .... for
   the honeymoon suite for the period you require.   AVAILABLE

5 The records must have accurate information so the staff
   should .... them regularly.   DATE

6 The customer has been taken ill so we've had a
   .... of the booking.   CANCEL

7 There's no one in room 507 at the moment and
   room 508 is also ....   OCCUPY

8 Hotels often don't .... specific
   rooms to specific guests until they arrive.   ALLOCATION

9 One of the first jobs to be done each day is to deal with
   the ....   CORRESPOND

10 When filling in the reservations form, please make sure
   that the .... are written clearly.   ENTER

6 Checking out

Fill in the missing words in the sentences below. Choose from the following. Use each verb once only and remember to put it into the correct form. (See example):

calculate	incur	liaise	settle
check out	issue	overcharge	sign for
dispute	itemize	return	vacate

At the end of their stay guests ...*check out*... at reception.

1 During their stay at a hotel, guests will .... charges for the services which they use in the hotel.

2 When a hotel guest eats in the hotel restaurant he/she will be asked to .... the meal before leaving.

3 Some hotels .... a luggage pass to show that payment has been received and the guest is free to leave.

4 Guests usually wish to see exactly what they are paying for, so the hotel should .... the bill to show each item separately.

5 Most hotels ask guests who are leaving to .... their rooms before lunchtime.

6 A computer also makes it much easier to .... any discount.

7 The receptionist will ask the guests to .... their bills before leaving the hotel.

8 The receptionist will .... any valuables which have been deposited for safe keeping.

9 Guests may .... a charge if they disagree with it.

10 In order to avoid problems the receptionist should .... with the other departments in the hotel.

11 Guests will be very unhappy if the hotel .... them and asks them to pay more.

7 Two-word nouns

Use the clues to fill in the missing letters in the two-word nouns below. There is one three-word noun!

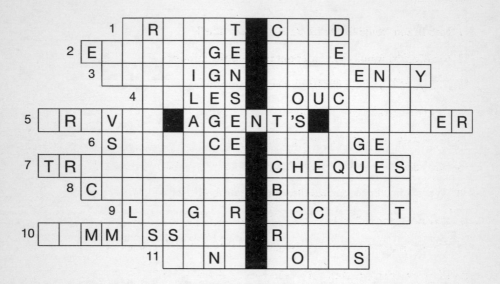

1 e.g. Barclaycard, Visa or Access.

2 The number of German Marks for American Dollars varies because of this.

3 Notes and coins from another country.

4 You sign this when you pay by 1 above.

5 Tourists who book through an agent will use this as a form of payment.

6 Often 10% or 15% added to the restaurant bill.

7 These cheques are often used by overseas customers.

8 The most modern system for preparing customers' bills.

9 Customers who regularly use the hotel may pay this monthly.

10 The level of administrative charges for changing money made by the hotel or bank.

11 Paper money.

8 Hotel facilities

The following guests have different wishes. In which section of the room information sheet should they look? Write the number of each guest next to the correct section. (See example):

1 Mrs Braun would like to have her blouse cleaned.

2 Mr Murphy wants to know about buses to the airport.

3 The McNeills would like breakfast in their room.

4 Christine Moore is feeling unwell.

5 Bob Dixon needs clean shoes for the morning.

6 Mrs Peterson has to be sure she gets up early tomorrow morning.

7 Fiona Frelimo wants to call her friend in Barcelona.

8 Tom Moshi would like a soft drink in his room.

9 Tim Morrison would like tea in his room before going for breakfast.

10 Mary Redman wants to know where to leave her car.

11 Eric and Jack wonder what they can do this evening.

12 David Blande wants to know the prices for different rooms.

INFORMATION

Room service	......	Tariffs	......
Telephone	......	Entertainment	......
Mini-bar	......	Shoe-cleaning service	......
Transport	......	Wake-up calls	......
Laundry	..1..	Garaging	......
Medical help	......	Early morning teas	......

9 Hotel accommodation

A   Match the plan on the left with its description on the right.

American Plan	bed only
Demi-pension	bed and breakfast
European Plan	bed, breakfast and lunch or dinner
Continental Plan	bed, breakfast, lunch and dinner

B   Write the number of each room type on the correct picture.

1 single   2 double   3 twin   4 adjoining   5 double en suite

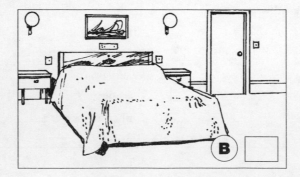

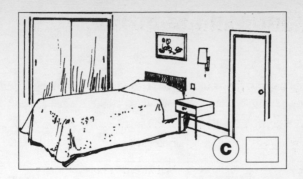

10 Out and about

Fill in the missing words in the sentences below. Choose from the following. Use each word once only, although there are more words than you need. Read the whole text first before trying to fill the gaps.

attractions	destination	festivals	nature
conveniences	displayed	galleries	resort
countryside	escorted	guides	ruins
courtesy	events	itinerary	scenery
cruise	excursions	locality	souvenirs
daily	ferries	museums	

Visitors arriving at the hotel will be interested to know what is on offer. Many hotels will arrange **(1)** .... tours by coach, or on foot to visit local **(2)** .... These may include historic **(3)** ...., art **(4)** .... or **(5)** .... where objects from the past can be seen.

Many people prefer to spend time out of doors and like to travel into the **(6)** ...., where they can enjoy and photograph the **(7)** .... The hotel can arrange half-day or full-day **(8)** .... and a detailed **(9)** .... will inform the guests of the exact route which will be taken. Guests are normally given some time to visit shops where they often buy **(10)** .... to remind them of their holiday when they return home. Alternatively, they may enjoy a **(11)** ....on a boat on a river or canal.

During the year there are many **(12)** .... taking place in the local area. Information about the time and place of these should be **(13)** .... in the hotel so that guests are aware of what is going on. The hotel can expect to be very busy when national or local **(14)** .... are taking place. Some of these are famous all over the world and attract many visitors.

11 Giving directions

Fill in the missing words in the sentences. There are several possibilities for some of them.

1

Turn right .... the bridge.

2

The newsagent is .... the bank.

3

Follow the road .... the school.

4

The ticket office is .... the book shop.

5

Go straight .... at the crossroads.

6

Walk .... the square.

7

You will see the tower .... your left.

8

Turn left .... Cuthbert Road. The Post Office is a little way .... the right.

9

Go .... Blair Avenue .... you see the church.

10
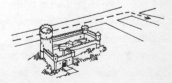

Take the second .... the right .... the castle.

12 Conferences 1

Fill in the following crossword.

Across

1 The number of days a conference will run.
2 The person who is invited to give a talk at a conference.
5 The person giving a talk is asked to .... the conference.
7 The document used by the hotel to list all the conference requirements. (8, 5)
8 It's held once a year.
9 The place where a conference is held.
10 If there are problems, it may be necessary to .... the conference to a later date.

Down

1 The people who come to a conference.
3 The dates have not been confirmed, they are only .... at the moment.
4 The week before the conference begins you have to .... all the arrangements with the conference organizers.

6   7

13 Conferences 2

Fill in the missing words in the sentences below. Choose from the following:

classroom	opening ceremonies	square metres
conference package	overhead projector	syndicate
conference programme	plenary	theatre
estimated attendance	seating capacity	
hospitality room	slide projector	

1 When describing the size of a room, the maximum number of people who can sit in the room is known as the ....

2 Organizers will probably require equipment for a conference; a .... to show photographs on the wall and an .... to show diagrams and text.

3 A conference hotel will probably calculate all the costs of the conference and offer the customer one total price called the ....

4 The size of rooms is given in ....

5 A conference begins with the ....

6 Guests are welcomed in the ....

7 The .... shows the guests what is happening where and when.

8 The expected number of guests is known as the ....

9 Conferences will require different room layouts. A room for all participants with only chairs is called .... style. If tables are also provided, it is referred to as .... style.

10 Smaller .... rooms for small groups of two to ten people may be needed too.

11 A session when all participants are present is known as a .... session.

14 A letter of complaint

The following extracts are from two different letters, a letter making a complaint and a letter of reply, but they have got mixed up. Put them in the right order to produce two correct letters.

1 When one of my guests arrived the waiter sat her at the wrong table. Later, the same waiter spilt a few drops of red wine on another guest's trousers. The final embarrassment was when the waiter presented the bill to one of my guests instead of me.

2 As a token of our regret I enclose a voucher for an evening meal for two people and hope to welcome you personally in the near future.

3 I am writing to complain about the service I recently received in your restaurant while on a business trip.

4 Yours sincerely
Pierre Lancel
Restaurant Manager

5 Yours faithfully
Raymond Strang
Sales Manager

6 Dear Sir/Madam

7 I had invited four clients to join me for lunch in your restaurant, where I had expected to receive the best service. Unfortunately, I have a number of complaints.

8 I am afraid that we were experiencing staffing problems during this period and had an inexperienced waiter working in the restaurant. He has since left and we are happy to say that we now have only fully qualified waiters serving our customers.

9 I feel that this is not the professional service which I expect from a top restaurant and I know that you will wish to ensure that it does not happen again.

10 Dear Mr Strang

11 I was very sorry to read of the problems which you experienced in our restaurant on your recent visit.

letter of complaint

☐ ☐ ☐ ☐ ☐ ☐

letter of reply

☐ ☐ ☐ ☐ ☐

15 The correct reply

Some guests are experiencing problems. Match each problem (1–14) with a suitable reply (a–n). Write the letters in the grid below.

1 This towel is damp.

2 The pillowcase is stained.

3 The shower curtain is torn.

4 I wanted a newspaper in my room.

5 The room is dusty.

6 There's a lot of noise on the telephone line.

7 The mirror is cracked.

8 I think the hairdrier is faulty.

9 The window is stuck.

10 My suitcase is still in my room.

11 The waste-paper basket is full.

12 This light bulb is too weak for reading.

13 The room is cold.

14 There's no ashtray in my room.

a) I'll get the chambermaid to clean it.

b) I'll have the heating turned up.

c) I'll get someone to open it.

d) I'll have it brought down.

e) I'll fetch you a dry one.

f) If you tell me which one you read I'll have it delivered.

g) I'll get you a clean one.

h) I'll have it replaced.

i) I'll have a stronger one fitted.

j) I'll have one brought to your room.

k) I'll have a new one put up.

l) I'll have it checked.

m) I'll call the operator and have it checked.

n) I'll get someone to empty it.

1	2	3	4	5	6	7	8	9	10	11	12	13	14

16 The bathroom

Look at the picture below and write the numbers 1–16 next to the correct word or words.

bath	......	pedal bin	......	tap	......
bath mat	......	plug	......	toilet	......
bath towel	......	shaver socket	......	toilet paper	......
glass	......	shower	......	wash basin	......
hand towel	......	shower curtain	......		
mirror	......	soap	......		

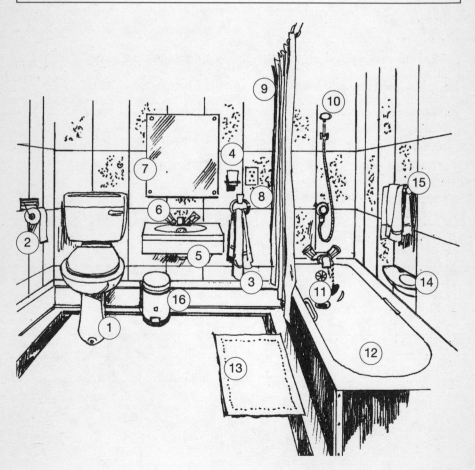

17 Furniture and fittings

Write the number of each drawing next to the correct word or words.

banister	......
blind	......
bookcase	......
ceiling	......
coat hanger	......
coat stand	......
cushion	......
curtains	......
curtain track	......
door handle	......
hairdrier	......
hinge	......
light switch	......
picture frame	......
skirting	......
wardrobe	......
window-sill	......

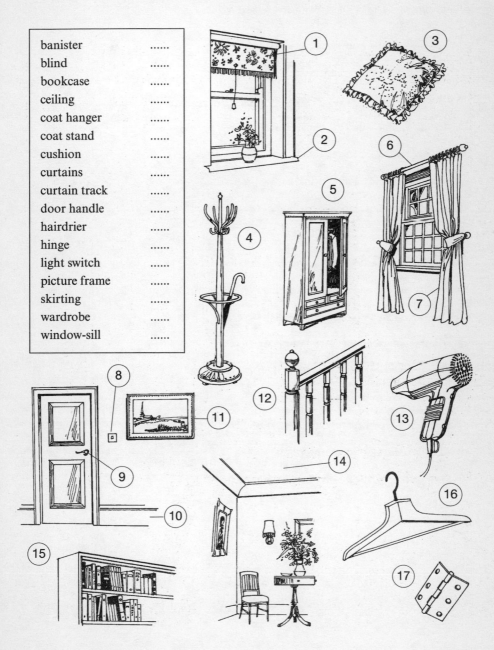

19

18 Name the place

Use the clues to fill in the missing letters. They are all places in hotel and catering establishments. The first letter is given for each one.

 1 The passageway between several rooms.   c _ _ _ _ _ _ _

 2 Guests can buy newspapers and magazines here.   k _ _ _ _

 3 Here you can sit outside your bedroom in the sun. b _ _ _ _ _ _

 4 Bedding and clothes are cleaned here.   l _ _ _ _ _ _

 5 Another word for foyer.   l _ _ _ _

 6 Guests can enjoy a long drink here.   c _ _ _ _ _ _ _ b _ _

 7 A bedroom on a ship.   c _ _ _ _

 8 Guests can leave suitcases here.   l _ _ _ l _ _ _ _ _ _

 9 It's cool and dark where the wine is kept!   c _ _ _ _ _

10 Guests can eat and drink outside here.   t _ _ _ _ _ _

11 Guests can sit comfortably and relax here.   l _ _ _ _ _

12 Climbing these to the sixth floor is tiring.   s _ _ _ _ _

13 Guests attending functions hang their coats here. c _ _ _ _ _ _ _ _

14 A quick way to reach the sixth floor.   l _ _ _

15 Food is cooked here.   k _ _ _ _ _ _

16 The place for a wedding reception.   b _ _ _ _ _ _ _ _ _ r _ _ _

17 Food is prepared here on board an aircraft.   g _ _ _ _ _

19 The building

Choose the word which best completes each sentence.

1 The restaurant is closed for two months while it is being ....
   a) renewed   b) remade   c) renovated   d) reformed

2 There will be ten new bedrooms when the builders finish the ....
   a) extension   b) extent   c) enlargement   d) utility

3 The chalets have everything a guest could require: they are ....
   a) self-catered   b) self-formed   c) self-made   d) self-contained

4 The building has fallen into a state of .... and now it needs a lot
   of work doing on it.
   a) despair   b) dispersal   c) disrepair   d) distress

5 This room is very quiet as it's not at the front of the hotel. It is ....
   a) back-looking   b) rear-facing   c) rear-looking   d) back-facing

6 The building is very old and the management have spent a lot of money
   .... the original features.
   a) restoring   b) installing   c) re-equipping   d) servicing

7 We apologize for any inconvenience caused during the .... of the
   new swimming pool.
   a) composition   b) formation   c) assembly   d) construction

8 The new restaurant is to be built on the .... of the old factory
   which was pulled down three years ago.
   a) site   b) position   c) ground   d) basis

9 The present location of the restaurant is not good and now Mr Martin is looking
   for new ....
   a) places   b) premises   c) estates   d) resorts

10 The .... around the hotel are beautifully planted with flowers.
   a) earth   b) floors   c) grounds   d) lands

20 Cleaning

Match the definitions (1–14) with the verbs (a–n).

1 Use a brush with a long handle to remove dry dirt from the floor.

2 Make the furniture and floors shine.

3 Clean the floor with water and a small brush.

4 Clean the floor with water and a cloth on a long handle.

5 Remove the dust from the shelf with a wet cloth.

6 Use water and soap powder to clean the linen.

7 Remove the soap with water.

8 Leave linen to stand in water for a few hours.

9 Clean the bed cover without water.

10 Clean the carpets, chairs and sofas with a machine.

11 Take all the used linen off the bed.

12 Put new soap and towels in the room.

13 Take away the waste.

14 Clean the carpets thoroughly.

a) dry clean
b) strip
c) sweep
d) wet mop
e) replenish
f) launder
g) vacuum
h) polish
i) deep clean
j) rinse
k) dispose of
l) soak
m) damp wipe
n) scrub

1	2	3	4	5	6	7	8	9	10	11	12	13	14

21 Mixed up letters

Rearrange the letters in brackets to form the correct words.

1 If silver isn't cleaned it will (rashitn) ....

2 Don't touch the glass window or you will leave (finpitsgrern) ....

3 Be careful if there is water on the floor as it will be (erslyppi) ....

4 Children having a bath often (shlasp) ....

5 Nasty smells in a room are known as (rsooud) ....

6 Don't use these (rasabevi) .... cleaning agents because they will scratch the surface.

7 Machines which make work quicker and easier are known as (loubar - avngsi) .... - .... devices.

8 In some areas of the country the water is hard and leaves (emil sleca) .... on baths.

9 Sometimes white cotton becomes yellow or grey and you can use (blchae) .... to whiten it again.

10 If red wine is spilt on the carpet, it will leave a (nsita) ....

11 Some waste, e.g. paper and empty cans, can be sold and, therefore, has a (salgeav) .... value.

12 Old pieces of metal may leave brownish (stur) .... marks on fabrics.

13 (entssvol) .... are used to remove marks which will not come out in water.

14 There will only be light (soageil) .... on carpets which are seldom used.

15 A special leather, which is used for cleaning windows, is called a (amchios) ....

22 Hotel systems 1

Fill in the missing words in the texts below. Choose from the following:

drains	humidity	sewer	U-bend
extractor	insulated	tank	ventilation
filters	pipes	thermostat	
grill	radiator		

Air

In large building complexes, fresh air will be supplied to rooms through an air-conditioning system. This provides (1) .... in each room so that guests can breathe comfortably and also controls the (2) .... so that the air doesn't contain too much moisture. In each room the opening to the air-conditioning system is covered with a (3) ....

In kitchens, steam and smells are sucked out by an (4) .... which contains (5) .... to remove any harmful gases.

Central heating

Heating may be underfloor or a (6) .... may be fitted to the wall in each room. The temperature in the room can be controlled by means of a (7) .... which will maintain a constant temperature. An efficient system will be well (8) .... so that energy is not lost.

Water

Water required for a building may be stored in a (9) .... Water is supplied to each room through (10) .... Waste water is removed through (11) .... which enter a main (12) .... outside the building.

Under baths and basins a (13) .... stops smells entering the room.

23 Hotel systems 2

Fill in the missing words in the text below. Choose from the following:

appliances	flex	overloaded	socket
current	fuse	plug	wiring
electrician	kilowatt hours		

Electricity

A hairdrier or an electric shaver are examples of electrical **(1)** ....
They have a **(2)** .... with a **(3)** .... at the end which fits into
a **(4)** .... in the wall. If there is a fault, the electricity supply will be cut by
a **(5)** ....

The amount of electricity used is measured in **(6)** .... The electrical **(7)** .... in Britain is 240 volts, while in many European countries
it is 220 volts. If too many pieces of equipment are connected to one supply, the
system may be **(8)** .... and there is a danger of fire. When problems arise, a qualified **(9)** .... should be called to check the
(10) ....

24 Fruit

Write the number of each picture next to the correct word or words.

apple	......
banana	......
blackcurrants	......
cherries	......
grapes	......
kiwi fruit	......
lemon	......
melon	......
orange	......
papaw	......
passion fruit	......
peach	......
raspberries	......
star fruit	......
strawberries	......

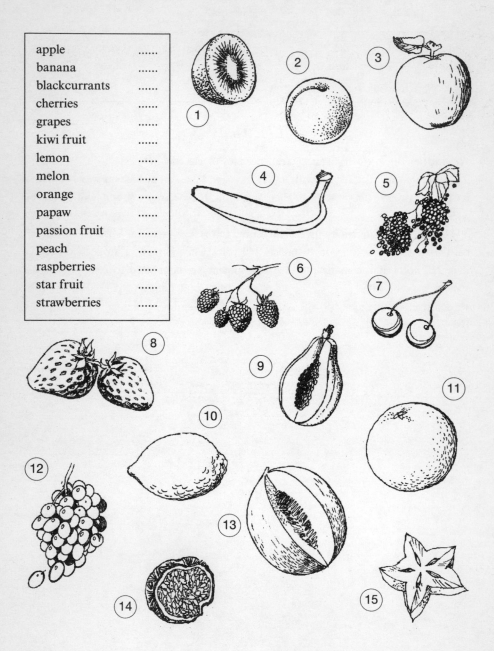

25 Vegetables

Write the number of each picture next to the correct word or words.

asparagus	......
aubergine	......
beetroot	......
butter-beans	......
carrot	......
cauliflower	......
courgette	......
French beans	......
leek	......
lettuce	......
okra	......
onion	......
peas	......
pepper	......
potato	......
radish	......
tomato	......

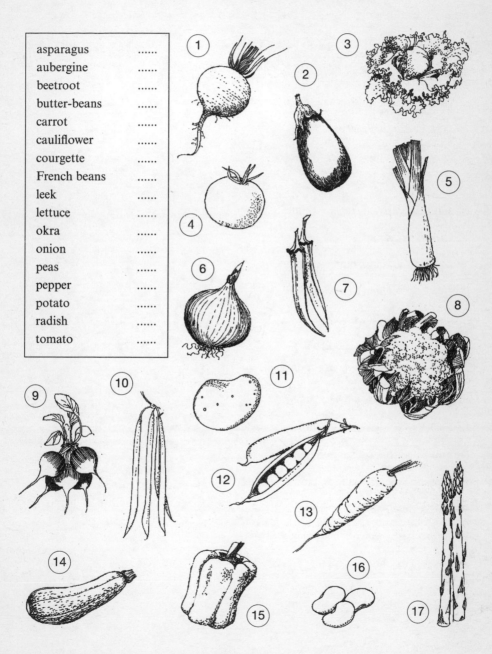

27

26 Classifications

Write one name for each of the following groups. (See example):

1 milk, cream, butter, yoghurt   d _dairy products_

2 almond, brazil, pistachio, cashew   n _ _ _

3 haricot beans, lentils, chick-peas, soya beans   p _ _ _ _ _

4 sage, parsley, thyme, basil   h _ _ _ _

5 ginger, cinnamon, cloves, turmeric   s _ _ _ _ _

6 pork, lamb, beef, mutton   m _ _ _

7 sultanas, currants, raisins, prunes   d _ _ _ _   f _ _ _ _

8 choux, flaky, puff, short   p a _ _ _ _ _ _

9 royal, glacé, satin, butter   i _ _ _ _ _

10 spaghetti, tagliatelle, ravioli, lasagne   p _ _ _ _

11 cod, perch, trout, salmon   f _ _ _

12 tea, coffee, orange juice, cola   b _ _ _ _ _ _ _ _

13 claret, rioja, chianti, sekt   w _ _ _ _

14 pheasant, grouse, venison, rabbit   g _ _ _

15 consommé, cock-a-leekie, broth, chowder   s _ _ _ _

16 gouda, stilton, camembert, parmesan   c _ _ _ _ _ _

17 mussels, oysters, scallops, prawns   s _ _ _ _ _ _

18 gingerbread, gateau, sponge, Swiss roll   c _ _ _ _

19 hollandaise, béchamel, mornay, Béarnaise   s _ _ _ _ _ _

20 wheat, rye, oats, barley   c e _ _ _ _ _ _

27 Taste

Fill in the missing words in the sentences below. Choose from the following:

bitter	delicious	hot	sour
bland	dry	rich	spicy
burnt	greasy	savoury	sweet

1 The skin of an orange tastes quite ....

2 Food cooked with chilli is ....

3 Food cooked with a lot of cream is very ....

4 Sugar and honey will make a dish ....

5 Indian food is ....

6 If you forget the salt and pepper the food will be ....

7 Lemon juice is ....

8 The main course cooked with salt and spices is ....

9 Too much fat used in cooking can make the dish ....

10 A dish without enough liquid is ....

11 A dish cooked to perfection will be ....

12 Toast cooked too long tastes ....

28 Cooking

Replace the words in **bold** type in sentences 1–14 with a single word from the list a–n.
Write the letters in the grid below.

1 The bread should be **cooked in dry heat in the oven** for about fifty minutes.

    a) dice

2 When roasting meat it should be **covered with melted fat regularly to keep the meat moist**.

    b) minced

3 **Decorate** the vegetables with some parsley.

    c) deep fry

4 Be very careful to **cook slowly, just below boiling point**.

    d) season

5 The meat for this recipe should be **cut into very small pieces**.

    e) poached

6 One method of cooking fish is to **cook** it **in lots of very hot fat**.

    f) baked

7 Could you **remove the skin and bones** from the fish before cooking it.

    g) garnish

8 When the potatoes are cooked you can **crush** them **to a pulp**.

    h) flavour

9 **Remove the outside skin of** the potatoes, please.

    i) defrost

10 Guests may like eggs which have been **broken into boiling water and vinegar**.

    j) mash

11 **Increase the temperature** completely before cooking the frozen chicken.

    k) peel

12 **Cut** the carrot **into small squares**.

    l) fillet

13 **Add salt and pepper** before serving the soup.

    m) simmer

14 You can **improve the taste of** the sauce with vanilla.

    n) basted

1	2	3	4	5	6	7	8	9	10	11	12	13	14

29 Utensils

Write the number of each drawing next to the word or words.

cake tin	......
chopping board	......
colander	......
cooling tray	......
dredger	......
frying pan	......
grater	......
ladle	......
mortar and pestle	......
parsley chopper	......
peeler	......
rolling pin	......
scissors	......
spatula	......
whisk	......

30 Phrasal verbs

Choose one definition from the box for each of the phrasal verbs in **bold** type in the sentences below.

become	continue	not have any left
become popular	find something in a	require
become rotten	book	take control
break a promise	learn	
cause (an object) to fall	look at again	
to the ground		

1 Stop wasting time and **get on with** your work ....

2 I've just been down to the store and we **are out of** flour.

 ....

3 If this milk isn't put in the fridge it will **go off** ....

4 If you're not sure of the quantities to use, **look** it **up** ....

5 When I've prepared the sauce, you can **take over** and complete the dish.

 ....

6 I've explained this once already but let's **go over** it to make sure you understand.

 ....

7 It looks very complicated but you'll soon **pick** it **up** ....

8 This machine has broken down again. We **could** really **do with** a new one.

 ....

9 If you continue to beat the cream, it will **turn into** butter.

 ....

10 Don't put that bowl there. Someone will **knock** it **over** ....

11 You promised to cook tomorrow and you can't **back out of** it now ....

12 I don't think beer with raspberry will ever **catch on**! Do you?

 ....

31 Hygiene

A Complete the table. (See example):

	Verb	Noun
1	to consume	*consumer/consumption*
2		cleanliness/cleaner
3	to poison	
4		infection
5	to disinfect	
6		sanitation/sanitizer
7		store/storage

B Now use words from the table to complete the following sentences.

1 Nowadays, it is necessary to .... knives, chopping boards and other pieces of catering equipment.

2 Kitchen staff are not allowed to .... alcohol while they are at work in the kitchen.

3 A .... can be added to water for cleaning the floor in order to remove germs.

4 The kitchen porter is responsible for hygiene and .... in the kitchen.

5 A cut on the finger must be cleaned very carefully to stop ....

6 A cool, dark, dry room is ideal to .... many dry food stuffs.

7 Frozen chickens must be defrosted completely before cooking to prevent food ....

32 A menu

Write each of the following dishes in the appropriate section of the menu.

Bavarian Apple Strudel	Herring and Apple Salad
Braised Leg of Lamb	Layered Vegetable Terrine
Broccoli with Hollandaise Sauce	Leaf Spinach with Diced Bacon
Cauliflower with Almonds	Okra and Courgettes in Lentil Sauce
Chef's Pâtés	Pear Hélène
Chicken Vichy	Potato Croquettes
Cold Chocolate Soufflé	Prawn and Orange Cocktail
Crème Caramel	Roast Pheasant en Croûte
Entrecôte Steak	Roast Potatoes
Escalope of Veal	Salad Marguery
French Onion Soup	Sweet Corn Chowder

THE WOODLAND

Menu

Appetisers

....
....

Salad

....
                    ....

Entrées

....
....
                    ....

Vegetarian Dishes

....

Vegetables and Side Dishes

....
....
                    ....

Desserts

....
....

Coffee

33 Service items

Fill in the following crossword. Each answer is an item found in the dining room.

Across

1 Used to open the wine bottle.
4 It hangs over the waiter's arm. (7, 5)
5 Fit the five candles in this.
6 Cheese is served on this. (6, 5)
7 The team of people working in the restaurant.
8 Carry the plates on this.
10 Carry the drinks on this.
11 White wine should be placed in this to reduce the temperature. (4, 6)
12 Put water or milk in this.
13 Cigarette smokers will need this.
14 Soup is served from this.
15 The fold marks in the tablecloth.
16 Salt and pepper set.
19 Serve the toast in a toast ....
20 Used to open a bottle of beer. (6, 6)
23 The guests use this to clean their fingers. (6, 4)
24 The best quality cloth for table linen.

Down

1 One word for plates, bowls, cups, etc.
2 One word for knives, forks, spoons, etc.
3 Another word for seasoning.
7 Bread is served in a bread ....
8 Used for lifting asparagus.
9 It stops the tea-leaves going into the cup. (3, 8)
10 It holds necessary items and provides a work surface for the waiters.
15 One place for one person at the table.
17 Sweets can be wheeled to the table on this.
18 Used to break the shells of nuts.
21 Serve a boiled egg in this. (3, 3)
22 Place this on the plate under the biscuits.

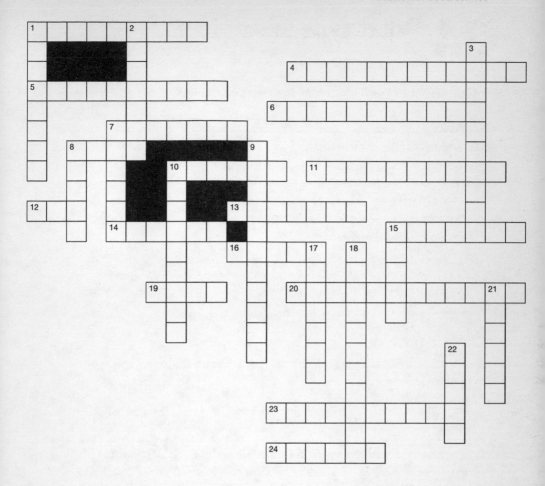

34 What type of service?

Write the number of each description next to the correct type of service.

Family	......	Gueridon	......	Plate	......	Silver	......
French	......	Mixed	......	Russian	......		

1 All the food is served in serving dishes which are placed on the table so that the guests can help themselves.

2 The food is put on the individual plates in the kitchen.

3 The guests help themselves from serving dishes which are held by the waiter.

4 The waiter serves the food at the table from a serving dish, using a spoon and fork.

5 The waiter serves the food from a serving dish using a fork and a spoon, while standing at a side table.

6 The waiter carves, fillets or cooks food at a side table and then places the food on a plate.

7 The main food is put on a plate in the kitchen and the vegetables are put on the table in serving dishes so that the guests can help themselves.

35 Giving service

Complete the dialogues below. Choose from the following. Use each line once only.

---

a) Ice and lemon with the gin, sir?

b) And what would you like to drink?

c) If you like fish, I can recommend the salmon steaks. The salmon is fresh from Scotland.

d) Dry or medium?

e) I'm sorry, but we're out of pineapple juice. We have orange or apple.

f) Are you ready to order, madam?

In the restaurant

WAITER: (1) ....

GUEST: I'm still looking. What can you recommend?

WAITER: (2) ....

GUEST: I'll have the salmon, then.

At the bar

WAITER: Yes, sir?

GUEST: A gin and tonic and a campari orange, please.

WAITER: (3) ....

GUEST: Yes, please. And a glass of white wine, please.

WAITER: (4) ....

GUEST: Dry, please.

In the snack bar

WAITER: Hello. Are you ready to order?

GUEST: Yes, I think so. We'll have one cheeseburger and one hamburger.

WAITER: (5) ....

GUEST: I'll have a pineapple juice and a mineral water for my girlfriend.

WAITER: (6) ....

GUEST: Orange, please.

36 A breakfast tray

Look at the picture below and write the numbers 1–12 next to the correct word or words.

butter dish	......	jam dish	......	small napkin	......
coffee pot	......	milk jug	......	sugar bowl	......
cup	......	saucer	......	teaspoon	......
dessert plate	......	small knife	......	toast plate	......

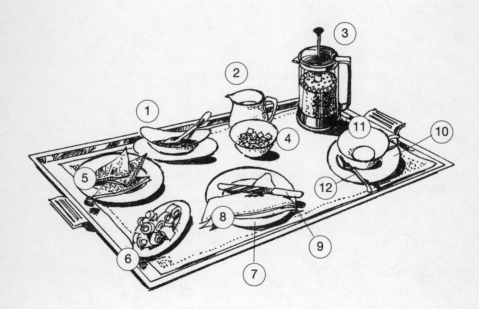

37 How to be polite

Read the direct phrases, then write them more politely. Choose from the following:

Could you	Please	Would you like me
Shall I	May I suggest	There's been a slight
I'm afraid	Would you mind	misunderstanding
Would you like	Actually	Just a moment

Direct	**More polite**
1 Wait a minute!	................................, please.
2 We haven't got any left.	.... we haven't got any left.
3 Sit down, please.	................................, take a seat.
4 You're wrong. I'm not the head waiter.	....................., I'm not the head waiter.
5 Do you want some water?	.... some water?
6 Move to another table!	.... moving to another table?
7 Confirm that tomorrow, please.	.... confirm that tomorrow, please?
8 Do you want a taxi?	.... to get you a taxi?
9 You've got the wrong date.	.... about the date.
10 Try this organic wine.	.... that you try this organic wine?
11 Do you want my help?	.... help you?

38 Safety first

Write the number of each picture next to the correct word or words.

accident report book	......
ambulance	......
bandages	......
cotton wool	......
fire alarm	......
fire bucket	......
fire escape	......
fire notice	......
first aid box	......
plasters	......
smoke detector	......
sprinkler	......
warning sign	......

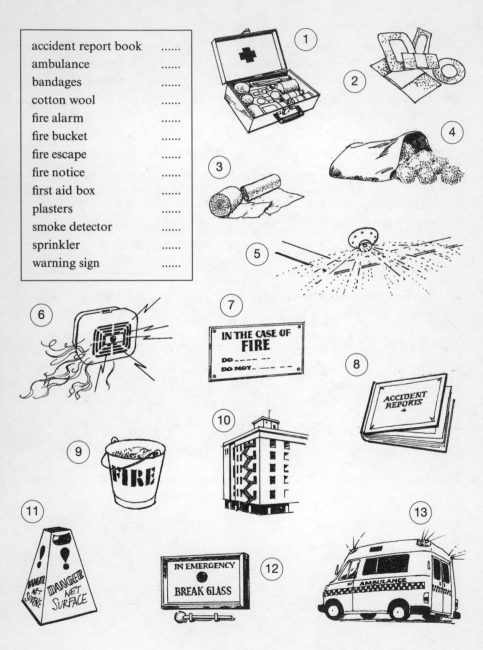

39 Fire procedures

Fill in the missing words in the fire notice for hotel employees. Choose from the following:

brigade	evacuate	lifts	smoke
drill	exit	raise	spread
doors	extinguish	safe	
enter	extinguisher		

1 Ask guests to check where the nearest fire .... is located as soon as they find their room.

2 There will be fire .... for everyone working in the hotel every six months.

3 All fire .... must be kept closed at all times as they will stop the .... of a fire.

4 If you see a small fire, you should try to .... it.

5 If it is an electrical fire, do not use a water fire ....

6 If it is a large fire, ... the alarm immediately.

7 Do not use the .... if there is a fire.

8 If there is a lot of .... , cover your mouth and nose with a handkerchief.

9 .... the building as quickly as possible.

10 Do not allow anyone to .... the building.

11 Check that everyone is ....

12 Phone for the fire ....

40 Unwelcome guests

Match the criminals (1–12) with the crimes (a–l). Write the letters in the grid below.

1 He stole a handbag in the foyer.

2 He said his name was Lord Pratt but after a three-week
   stay in the hotel he disappeared without paying.

3 There was some money lying on the desk so she took it.

4 He sexually attacked a woman.

5 He was holding a gun as he told the cashier to give
   him all the money.

6 She sold heroin to someone in the hotel.

7 He drank too much whisky and made a lot of noise.

8 She made false copies of American dollars.

9 He set fire to the hotel because he was angry with
   the manager.

10 He attacked and robbed a lady in the corridor.

11 He broke the toilet and basin and sprayed paint on
   the wall.

12 He broke a window at night and stole valuable items
   and money.

a) forger

b) drug pusher

c) burglar

d) drunk

e) opportunist

f) rapist

g) mugger

h) arsonist

i) thief

j) vandal

k) armed robber

l) fraudster

1	2	3	4	5	6	7	8	9	10	11	12

41 Word building 2

The word in capitals at the end of each sentence can be used to form a word that fits suitably in the blank space. Fill each blank in this way. (See example):

The hotel asks guests not to leave ...... *valuable* ...... pieces of jewellery in the room.   VALUE

1 This area of the hotel is only for ....
   personnel.   AUTHORITY

2 The management must do all it can to
   .... the hotel guests.   PROTECTION

3 Burglar alarms often work as a .... and
   stop burglars even thinking about breaking in.   DETER

4 The receptionist called the police because there was a
   strange woman behaving very .... SUSPICIOUS

5 The management hope that computerized door locks
   will .... thieves from getting into
   hotel rooms.   PREVENTION

6 It's always possible that the money has been stolen by
   a .... member of staff.   HONEST

7 Valuable items should be marked with
   .... codes which the thief cannot see
   but which can be seen under UV light.   VISIBLE

8 Every member of staff should be alert and if they
   .... anything strange they should
   report it immediately.   OBSERVATION

9 Never accept a cheque without .... IDENTIFICATION

10 Before you leave the building you must make sure that
   all the doors are .... locked.   SECURE

11 Members of staff who prove themselves to be
   .... will be given more responsibility. TRUST

42 Legal words

Use the clues on the left to fill in the missing letters in the legal words on the right.

1 The laws which businesses must observe.   _ EGISLATIO_

2 To be responsible if someone is injured   _ IABL _
   in the restaurant.

3 To refuse to let someone come into the bar.   _ XCLUD _

4 Someone who buys something.   _ URCHASE _

5 Someone who sells something.   _ ENDO _

6 An official agreement between two parties.   _ ONTRAC _

7 The person who owns the hotel.   _ ROPRIETO _

8 You pay this if you are caught breaking the law.   _ IN _

9 You mustn't sell alcohol to someone under
   the age of 18 because it's . . .   _ ROHIBITE _

10 Official permission to sell alcohol.   _ ICENC _

11 The person who has permission
   to sell alcohol.   _ ICENSE _

12 Allow someone to enter a club.   _ DMI _

13 To enter the private areas of the hotel   _ RESPAS _
   without permission.

14 The length of time spent in prison.   _ ENTENC _

15 Leaving dangerous chemicals where
   children could find them.   _ EGLIGENC _

16 The police will do this to law breakers.   _ ROSECUT _

17 You must report serious accidents. It's . . .   _ OMPULSOR _

43 What do they mean?

Choose the best meaning for each of the following phrases.

1 to comply with the law
  a) to do things as the law states
  b) to change parts of the law
  c) to complain about the law

2 unfit for human consumption
  a) the food should not be eaten
  b) the food is good for giving energy
  c) the food is being prepared

3 must be used solely for the purpose of
  a) should not be used too often
  b) should only be used for
  c) must not be used

4 intoxicating spirit
  a) drinks which contain alcohol
  b) drinks which have over 20% alcohol
  c) drinks which have over 30% alcohol

5 to be needlessly exposed to risk
  a) some machines could be dangerous
  b) you mustn't show problems
  c) there are unnecessary dangers which could easily be removed

6 to sustain personal injury
  a) to get an insurance policy
  b) to be hurt
  c) to get promotion

7 to make available for inspection
  a) to find time to maintain the machines
  b) to arrange to clean the machine
  c) to let inspectors see what they wish

8 in the event of an accident
  a) after an accident
  b) if there is an accident
  c) avoid accidents

9 persons frequenting the premises
  a) people cleaning the hotel
  b) people outside
  c) people using the hotel

10 a breach of contract
  a) an action which breaks a contract
  b) an action which cancels a contract
  c) an action which is included in a contract

11 to be legally obliged to do something
  a) you must do it
  b) it is allowed to do it
  c) you shouldn't do it

44 Carriers of disease

Write the number of each picture next to the correct word or words.

bedbug	......
chicken	......
cockroach	......
flea	......
fly	......
mosquito	......
moth	......
mouse	......
pigeon	......
rat	......
sparrow	......
spider	......
starling	......
wasp	......

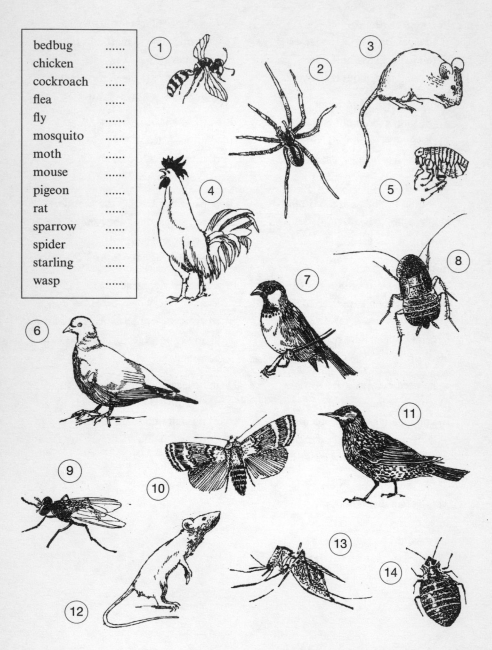

45 Health and hygiene

A Match the verbs in the left-hand column with a word or phrase from the right-hand column. (See example):

harbour	infection
come	diseases
dispose	separate
transmit	into contact with
spread	pain
keep	germs
relieve	of waste
prevent	food
contaminate	accidents

B Fill in the missing words in the sentences below. Choose from the combinations in A.

Don't leave wet towels or cloths lying in a warm corner because this is how you will ....*harbour germs*.... .

1 Don't spray fly killer in the kitchen or you could .... the ....

2 If you are stung by a wasp, put this cream on to .... the ....

3 To .... happening don't leave things lying on the floor.

4 If you are handling dirty linen, wash your hands regularly so that you don't
....

5 If you .... animal droppings,
please wash your hands immediately.

6 To .... safely, place it in these plastic bags and tie
them securely.

7 In the fridge please .... raw meat and cheese ....

8 In tropical climates it is possible to .... some .... drinking
water.

46 Employment

Fill in the crossword. Each answer is to do with employment.

Across

1 A person who is in employment.
4 This type of job is only for a few hours a week. (4, 4)
7 The extra money left by guests.
8 If you work extra hours you get paid this.
10 People who are happy at work have job . . .
12 The manager appointed him to the . . . of head waiter.
13 The more jobs you do and the longer you work, the more of this you get.
15 The extra money that workers get from the management as a special thank you.
16 The meeting when you discuss a possible new job.
18 If you decide to leave the job, you have to . . .
20 A hotel which is very busy in the summer will need . . . workers.
21 To get the best results from workers, the personnel manager must . . .
   them.
23 Before you go to discuss a new job you make an . . .
25 This money is paid to people who have reached the official age to stop working.
26 Someone who has written to ask for a job.

Down

1 The person or company who employs you.
2 To find suitable people and employ them is to . . .
3 This is a percentage of what you can earn which you pay to the State. (6, 3)
5 When people reach the official age to stop working they . . .
6 People have these if they have studied and passed professional exams.
7 Another way of saying 'to employ'. (4, 2)
9 When the manager has found a new chef, he will . . . him to the position.
10 The housekeeper has to . . . the work of the cleaning staff.
11 People who are paid weekly are paid . . .
14 When you move up to a more senior position, you get . . .
17 The time that you start work is the time you come . . . (2, 4)
19 A word for all the people who work in the hotel or restaurant.
22 Write a letter and . . . for the job if you are interested.
24 When you work, you . . . money.

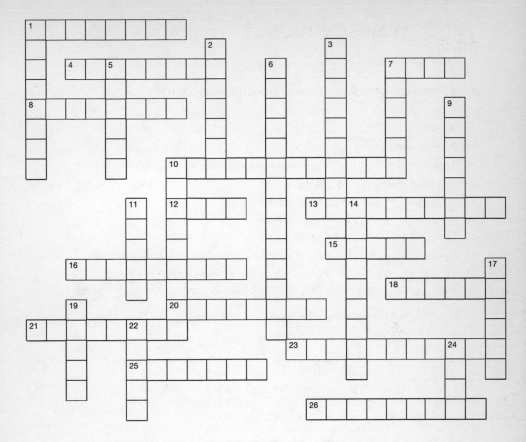

47 Whose job is it?

Write the number of each description next to the correct person.

advance reservations	chef	pantry maid .....
clerk	dispense bartender	pastry cook .....
banqueting	enquiry clerk	personnel manager .....
manager	head waiter	receptionist .....
cashier	housekeeper	waitress .....
cellarman	house porter	

1 Someone has to make sure that everything in the guests' rooms is in order.

2 Mr and Mrs Murphy would like to discuss arrangements for their daughter's wedding reception.

3 The guests' bills need to be prepared.

4 Someone has to make sure there is enough wine, beer and spirits.

5 The sheets and towels have to be taken upstairs.

6 Four guests have just entered the restaurant.

7 The waiter wants wine and beer for his tables.

8 A special cake should be made for the function.

9 The busy summer season is approaching and more staff are required.

10 Someone should plan the cooking times for dinner.

11 This letter booking two rooms for next month needs a reply.

12 Someone has to welcome guests and complete the registration form.

13 Someone has to prepare early morning teas.

14 Guests at table 8 are ready to order.

15 A lady on the telephone wants to know if there is a room available at the weekend.

48 Job advertisements

Find words or phrases in the advertisements below which mean the following.

1 only for important people ....

2 an applicant's list of qualifications and experience ....

3 equipped ....

4 minimum of ....

5 looking for ....

6 not newly started ....

7 chances of promotion ....

8 extras to wages/salaries ....

9 applicants ....

10 able to develop new ideas ....

11 at the start ....

12 salary/wages higher than at other hotels ....

GREAT HOTEL

Receptionists

This exclusive hotel in the heart of the city is seeking candidates who are enthusiastic and innovative. We offer excellent benefits, great prospects and competitive pay. Candidates must have at least two years' experience.
Please call Linda Bolam on 0192 13579

CHEF

Enthusiastic and energetic chef required to initially work with chef/proprietor and later take over established restaurant. The kitchens are fitted out to the highest standard. We are locally known for our fish specialities. Own flat available.
Write enclosing C.V. to John Bloggs, The Woodlands, Wayside Road, Oakton MN13 9EJ

49 Positive thinking

Here are thirty words or phrases which are used to describe hotels and their facilities. Write each word or phrase in the appropriate column below. There are six words in each.

appetizing	grand	popular family
beachside	gourmet	romantic
beautifully decorated	highly recommended	spacious
bright	home cooked	tastefully furnished
central	hospitable	traditional
cheerful	ideally placed	tranquil
conveniently situated	majestic	welcoming
delicious	mouth watering	well appointed
elegant	peaceful	well located
nourishing	picturesque setting	well run

Rooms
....
....
....
....
....
....

Location
....
....
....
....
....
....

Food
....
....
....
....
....
....

Hotel
....
....
....
....
....
....

Atmosphere
....
....
....
....
....
....

50 Marketing

Choose the word which best completes each sentence.

1 One way to find out about your customers, their needs and how much money they are willing to spend is to ask them to complete ....
a) an inquiry form   b) a questionnaire   c) a booking form.

2 To be successful the outlet must .... the needs of the customer.
a) satisfy   b) provide   c) decide

3 One way to tell the public that the outlet exists is by ....
an advertisement in the local newspaper.
a) giving   b) advertising   c) placing

4 Some companies may decide to advertise all over the country in an advertising
....
a) campaign   b) survey   c) action

5 When there isn't much business, the restaurant may advertise a special
.... to increase sales.
a) order   b) offer   c) market

6 If food is attractively displayed, customers will be .... to buy.
a) forced   b) treated   c) tempted

7 It is up to the staff to create a good .... of the restaurant.
a) image   b) side   c) reflection

8 Free badges, hats, T-shirts, and book matches are examples of
.... material.
a) selling   b) potential   c) promotional

9 A restaurant will lose sales if it gets bad .... in local newspapers
after an accident.
a) publication   b) public   c) publicity

10 On the other hand, a newspaper .... about the excellent food and
service will increase sales.
a) story   b) advice   c) article

11 In large towns you have to .... with other outlets.
a) compete   b) competitor   c) competition

51 Computer systems

Rearrange the letters in brackets to form the correct words.

1 A computer is an ideal machine for (stngior) .... information about reservations.

2 Once the information about reservations has been entered, other (licappionsat) .... can be added.

3 In both the back office and at reception the information can be viewed through (DUVs) ....

4 The reservations clerk can type in information using a (yekdboar) ....

5 The reservations clerk can then see the information on a (enescr) ....

6 In order to speed up the process and simplify the system, the hotel will use (cesdo) ....

7 The necessary information for reservations will be shown in a (mune) .... display.

8 It is only sometimes necessary to have written information on paper in the form of a (proutint) ....

9 If information were lost it would be catastrophic so all information should be (edbakc pu) .... at regular intervals and stored on (skid) .... or tape.

10 Some hotel groups have designed their computer systems to (infactere) .... with telex, airline networks and travel agents.

11 When a guest registers at the hotel, the information can be entered straight away and later (callreed) .... if requested.

12 A (ordw-pressingoc) .... - .... facility on a computer allows office staff to quickly produce letters.

13 Computers are also used in bars where exact amounts of spirits are dispensed by (opctis) ....

14 In the restaurant or bar, customers' bills can be calculated quickly and accurately at the electronic (pinto fo selas) ....

15 It is also possible for customers' orders to be keyed into the computer at the table through a hand-held (minalrte) ....

16 Linen control has been greatly improved with an identification system which uses (bra desco) ....

17 Messages can be sent and received by hotel staff and guests by using (elonictrec mali) ....

18 Written messages as well as drawings and diagrams can be sent through the telephone system using a (xfa) ....

19 Many hotels are trying to increase security by using a (kye ardc temssy) ....
.... which records every time a lock is opened and by whom.

52 Office items

Write the number of each picture next to the correct word or words.

bulldog clip	......
calculator	......
desk diary	......
diskette	......
hole punch	......
notepad	......
planner	......
printer ribbon	......
ring binder	......
ruler	......
stapler	......
suspension file	......
trays	......
window envelope	......

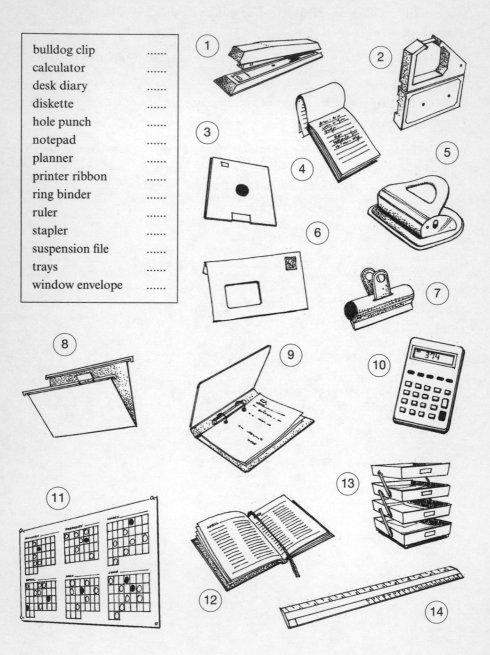

53 At work in the office

Fill in the missing prepositions in the sentences. Choose from the following. Some of the prepositions are used more than once.

about	for	from	of	off	on	out	to	with

1 Could you take care .... the seating arrangements for the conference?

2 Mrs Brown has complained .... the food .... the manager.

3 The number of staff depends .... the season.

4 Something seems to have happened .... this plant. It's dead!

5 We still haven't heard .... those clients about what flowers they want.

6 I can't find the keys and I've looked .... them everywhere.

7 I'm relying .... you to sort .... this problem peacefully.

8 I'll think .... how to promote your idea of a Japanese night, and we'll discuss it later.

9 We should provide our cleaners .... new uniforms.

10 I'm glad you reminded me .... the meeting. I'd forgotten!

11 Any telephone costs will be added .... the bill.

12 Chef won't put up .... any nonsense in the kitchen.

13 These new computer key cards should cut down .... electricity costs as they turn the lights .... as soon as the guests go out.

14 The manager is very pleased .... this month's sales figures.

15 Our restaurant is famous .... its fish dishes.

16 It's been so cold that there's been no demand .... soft drinks.

54 Handling Stock

A Fill in the bin card headings. Choose from the following:

balance	item	price	suppliers
date	maximum	quantity	type
in	minimum	reference	unit

................: Sherry			................: 75 cl bottle	
................: Amontillado			................: £2.53	
....	....	....	**Out**	....
1st Oct	JB	24		24
2nd Oct	BP		6	18
4th Oct	JB		3	15
6th Oct	JB	24		39
7th Oct	BP		10	29
.... stock: 48			.... stock: 8	
Re-order point: 24			...................: Classic Wine Importers	
Re-order ....: 24			Ltd	

B Update the card with the following information.

1 On 8th October 8 bottles were issued by John Bridges.
2 On 12th October 24 bottles were received from the suppliers by John Bridges.
3 Barbara Palm took 10 bottles on 13th October.

55 Business documentation

Use the clues on the left to fill in the missing letters in the words on the right.

1 A member of staff writes this when goods
are running short and are now required.   REQU _ _ _ _ _ _ _

2 This information is then sent to an external
supplier as an official . . .   OR _ _ _

3 When the goods are delivered, this list of
goods is often enclosed.   DE _ _ _ _ _ _ N _ _ _

4 After delivery the supplier sends this list
of goods giving quantity and price.   IN _ _ _ _ _ _

5 If you pay within seven days, you can often get a . . .   C _ _ _ DI _ _ _ _ _ _

6 If you buy regularly from the local baker he may
allow you a . . .   TR _ _ _ DI _ _ _ _ _ _

7 At the end of the month most suppliers send out
this list of everything bought and all money paid.   ST _ _ _ _ _ _ _

8 If goods have to be returned to the supplier he will
send this to adjust the amount of money due.   C _ _ _ _ _ N _ _ _

9 This will be sent if a customer doesn't pay
his/her account.   R _ _ _ _ DER

56 Facts and figures

Write the number of each picture next to the correct word or words.

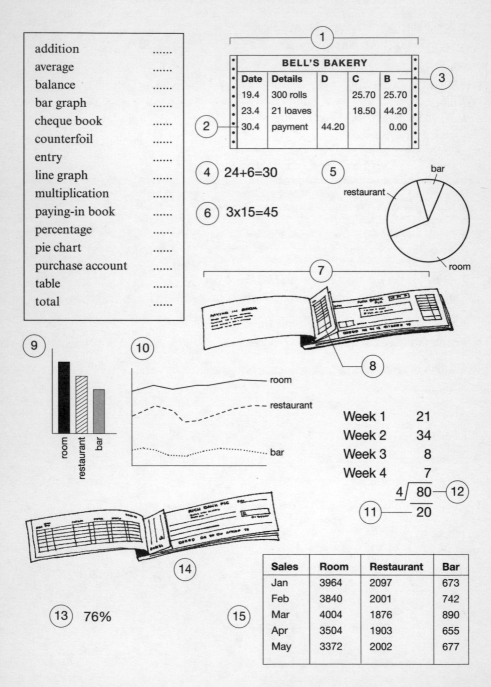

addition ......
average ......
balance ......
bar graph ......
cheque book ......
counterfoil ......
entry ......
line graph ......
multiplication ......
paying-in book ......
percentage ......
pie chart ......
purchase account ......
table ......
total ......

1

BELL'S BAKERY

Date	Details	D	C	B
19.4	300 rolls		25.70	25.70
23.4	21 loaves		18.50	44.20
30.4	payment	44.20		0.00

2 **3**

4 24+6=30   **5**

6 3x15=45

pie chart labels: bar, restaurant, room

7 **8**

9 bar graph: room, restaurant, bar

10 line graph: room, restaurant, bar

Week 1   21
Week 2   34
Week 3   8
Week 4   7

$4\overline{)80}$ — **12**

11 — 20

14

13 76%   **15**

Sales	Room	Restaurant	Bar
Jan	3964	2097	673
Feb	3840	2001	742
Mar	4004	1876	890
Apr	3504	1903	655
May	3372	2002	677

57 Accountancy terms

Fill in the missing words in the sentences below. Choose from the following:

cash float	debit	petty cash book
credit	debtors	posted
credit customer accounts	double entry	purchase ledger
creditors	payroll	visitors' paid-outs

1 Most companies use a system of accounting known as
   ....

2 This divides the page into two columns which are called
   .... and ....

3 Suppliers who have not yet received payment for goods which they have already
   delivered are ....

4 Customers who have not yet paid their bills are ....

5 The accounts of suppliers to the hotel are kept in the ....

6 The accounts of customers are known as ....

7 When figures are moved from one account to another they are
   ....

8 All the information needed to pay staff wages and salaries is on the
   ....

9 Small amounts of cash which are paid out are recorded in the
   ....

10 Small items of cash which are paid out on behalf of a guest are called
   ....

11 At the start of each day the bar and restaurant staff are given a fixed amount of
   cash which is called a ....

58 Final accounts

Match the words (1–13) on the left with their definitions (a–m) on the right. Write the letters in the grid below.

1	Profit and Loss Account	a)	Includes cash in the safe and in the bank.
2	Trading Account	b)	Bills which will never be paid.
3	Balance Sheet	c)	When sales equal costs – no profit or loss.
4	Fixed assets	d)	Includes rent, telephone, gas, advertising.
5	Current assets	e)	Shows the gross profit at the end of the year.
6	Long term liabilities	f)	Furniture, kitchen equipment, crockery, etc.
7	Current liabilities	g)	Food, liquor, and tobacco still in store.
8	Bad debts	h)	A statement at the end of the year showing how the company is financed.
9	Depreciation	i)	Borrowed money which will be paid back over a long period of time.
10	Budget	j)	Money which will be paid to suppliers soon.
11	Overheads	k)	Reduction in value of machines and furniture over several years.
12	Stock	l)	Shows the net profit after electricity, rent, stationery, etc. has been deducted.
13	Break-even point	m)	Planned financial figures for the future.

1	2	3	4	5	6	7	8	9	10	11	12	13

59 Nationalities and currencies

A Complete the table.

Country	People	Language	Currency
Canada		English/French	
Germany		German	
Italy			Lire (ITL)
	Japanese	Japanese	
	Australians		Dollar (AUD)
		Russian	Rouble (RUR)
Switzerland		German/French/ Italian	
United Kingdom	British	English	Pound (GBP)
United States of America	Americans		
Sweden	Swedes		Krona (SEK)
	French		Franc (FRF)

B Now use the words from the table to complete the following sentences.

1 What is the exchange rate for American dollars into French ....?

2 You're from Italy! I'm afraid I don't speak ....

3 These guests are from Germany and I can't speak ....

4 The guests in room 147 are ...., from Japan.

5 How many .... will I get for one pound when I go to Sweden?

6 Our American guests from the .... want to pay in dollars.

7 Can we accept .... from our Russian guests?

8 Can you tell me the rate of the Swiss .... today?

British English and American English

British English	American English
accommodation	accommodations
alter	change
aubergine	egg-plant
barman	bartender
bill (for food)	check
biscuit	cookie
cheque	check
colour	color
courgette	zucchini
cupboard, wardrobe	closet
curtains	drapes
enquiry	inquiry
fill in	fill out
form	blank/form
fridge	icebox
hairdrier	hair dryer
holiday	vacation
interconnecting	adjoining
labour	labor
lager	beer
licence	license
lift	elevator
luggage	baggage/luggage
main course	entrée
note (paper money)	bill
page boy	bell boy, bell hop, page
post	mail
provisional	unconfirmed
pub	saloon/bar
purse	pocket book
reception	front desk/front office
receptionist	clerk, desk clerk
rubbish	garbage/trash
shop	store

spirit	liquor
starter	appetiser
sunglasses	shades
syndicate room	conference room
tap	faucet
taxi	cab
toilet	bathroom, restroom, washroom
traveller's cheques	travelers checks
venue	locale
waiter	waiter/food server
washbasin	sink

Answers

Section 1:
THE FRONT OFFICE

TEST 1

binoculars	11
cap	5
carrier bag	1
compact	7
doll	6
glasses	14
glove	9
keys	10
lipstick	13
pocket diary	8
purse	4
ski stick	15
tie	12
toilet bag	2
umbrella	3

TEST 2
1 a 2 i 3 h 4 g 5 d 6 e 7 c 8 f
9 j 10 b

TEST 3
1 (b) foyer
2 (b) deal with
3 (c) regulars
4 (a) safe deposit
5 (c) clientele
6 (a) register
7 (c) arrivals
8 (c) pass
9 (a) pigeon hole
10 (b) chance
11 (d) no shows
12 (d) occupancy

TEST 4
Letter of reservation: 5, 3, 7, 8, 2, 1

Dear Sir/Madam
I would like to reserve four single rooms from 19th to 24th November 19– for four of our managers.

The rooms should be booked in the names of John Brown, Mary Black, Bill Franks and Ann Jones.

Could you please inform me of your rates and whether you offer discounts for company bookings.

I look forward to receiving your confirmation.
Yours faithfully
Susan Peacock
Secretary

Letter of confirmation: 11, 6, 9, 4, 10

Dear Ms Peacock
Thank you for your letter of 16th September 19–. We are very pleased that you have chosen to use our hotel for your four managers who will be in Anyton from 19th to 24th November 19– .

I would like to confirm your reservation for four single rooms for these dates. We are happy to be able to offer you our corporate rates, which you will find in the enclosed leaflet.

We look forward to receiving our guests.
Yours sincerely
Peter Black
Reservations Clerk

TEST 5
1 provisional
2 confirmed
3 overbooked
4 availability
5 update
6 cancellation
7 unoccupied
8 allocate
9 correspondence
10 entries

TEST 6
1 incur
2 sign for
3 issue
4 itemize

5 vacate
6 calculate
7 settle
8 return
9 dispute
10 liaise
11 overcharges

TEST 7
1 credit card
2 exchange rate
3 foreign currency
4 sales voucher
5 travel agent's voucher
6 service charge
7 travellers cheques
8 computer billing
9 ledger account
10 commission rate
11 bank notes

Section 2:
HOTEL SERVICES

TEST 8
1 Laundry
2 Transport
3 Room service
4 Medical help
5 Shoe cleaning service
6 Wake-up calls
7 Telephone
8 Mini-bar
9 Early morning teas
10 Garaging
11 Entertainment
12 Tariffs

TEST 9
(A)
American Plan – bed, breakfast, lunch and dinner
Demi-pension – bed, breakfast and lunch or dinner
European Plan – bed only
Continental Plan – bed and breakfast

(B)
A 3 B 2 C 1 D 5 E 4

TEST 10

1 escorted
2 attractions
3 ruins
4 galleries
5 museums
6 countryside
7 scenery
8 excursions
9 itinerary
10 souvenirs
11 cruise
12 events
13 displayed
14 festivals

TEST 11

1 at / before
2 opposite
3 past
4 beside / next to
5 on/ahead
6 across
7 on
8 into, along / down / up, on
9 along / down / up, until / till
10 on, after

TEST 12

Across

1 duration
2 speaker
5 address
7 function sheet
8 annual
9 venue
10 postpone

Down

1 delegates
3 provisional
4 finalize
6 lectern
7 flipchart

TEST 13

1 seating capacity
2 slide projector, overhead projector
3 conference package
4 square metres
5 opening ceremonies
6 hospitality room
7 conference programme
8 estimated attendance
9 theatre, classroom

10 syndicate
11 plenary

TEST 14

Letter of complaint: 6, 3, 7, 1, 9, 5

Dear Sir/Madam

I am writing to complain about the service I recently received in your restaurant while on a business trip.

I had invited four clients to join me for lunch in your restaurant, where I had expected to receive the best service. Unfortunately, I have a number of complaints.

When one of my guests arrived the waiter sat her at the wrong table. Later, the same waiter spilt a few drops of red wine on another guest's trousers. The final embarrassment was when the waiter presented the bill to one of my guests instead of me.

This is not the professional service which I expect from a top restaurant and I know that you will wish to ensure that it does not happen again.

Yours faithfully
Raymond Strang
Sales Manager

Letter of reply: 10, 11, 8, 2, 4

Dear Mr Strang

I was very sorry to read of the problems which you experienced in our restaurant on your recent visit.

I am afraid that we were experiencing staffing problems during this period and had an inexperienced waiter working in the restaurant. He has since left and we are happy to say that we now have only fully qualified waiters serving our customers.

As a token of our regret I enclose a voucher for an evening meal for two people and hope to welcome you personally in the near future.

Yours sincerely
Pierre Lancel
Restaurant Manager

TEST 15

1 e 2 g 3 k 4 f 5 a 6 m 7 h 8 l
9 c 10 d 11 n 12 i 13 b 14 j

Section 3:
HOUSEKEEPING

TEST 16

bath	12
bath mat	13
bath towel	15
glass	4
hand towel	3
mirror	7
pedal bin	16
plug	11
shaver socket	8
shower	10
shower curtain	9
soap	14
tap	6
toilet	1
toilet paper	2
wash basin	5

TEST 17

banister	12
blind	1
bookcase	15
ceiling	14
coat hanger	16
coat stand	4
cushion	3
curtains	7
curtain track	6
door handle	9
hairdrier	13
hinge	17
light switch	8
picture frame	11
skirting	10
wardrobe	5
window-sill	2

TEST 18

1 corridor
2 kiosk
3 balcony
4 laundry
5 lobby

6 cocktail bar
7 cabin
8 left luggage
9 cellar
10 terrace
11 lounge
12 stairs
13 cloakroom
14 lift
15 kitchen
16 banqueting room
17 galley

TEST 19

1 (c) renovated
2 (a) extension
3 (d) self-contained
4 (c) disrepair
5 (b) rear-facing
6 (a) restoring
7 (d) construction
8 (a) site
9 (b) premises
10 (c) grounds

TEST 20

1 c 2 h 3 n 4 d 5 m 6 f 7 j 8 l
9 a 10 g 11 b 12 e 13 k 14 i

TEST 21

1 tarnish
2 fingerprints
3 slippery
4 splash
5 odours
6 abrasive
7 labour-saving
8 lime scale
9 bleach
10 stain
11 salvage
12 rust
13 solvents
14 soilage
15 chamois

TEST 22

1 ventilation
2 humidity
3 grill
4 extractor
5 filters
6 radiator
7 thermostat
8 insulated
9 tank

10 pipes
11 drains
12 sewer
13 U-bend

TEST 23

1 appliances
2 flex
3 plug
4 socket
5 fuse
6 kilowatt hours
7 current
8 overloaded
9 electrician
10 wiring

Section 4:
FOOD AND DRINK

TEST 24

apple	3
banana	4
blackcurrants	5
cherries	7
grapes	12
kiwi fruit	1
lemon	10
melon	13
orange	11
papaw	9
passion fruit	14
peach	2
raspberries	6
star fruit	15
strawberries	8

TEST 25

asparagus	17
aubergine	2
beetroot	1
butter beans	16
carrot	13
cauliflower	8
courgette	14
French beans	10
leek	5
lettuce	3
okra	7
onion	6
peas	12
pepper	15
potato	11
radish	9
tomato	4

TEST 26

1 dairy products
2 nuts
3 pulses
4 herbs
5 spices
6 meat
7 dried fruit
8 pastries
9 icings
10 pasta
11 fish
12 beverages
13 wines
14 game
15 soups
16 cheeses
17 seafood
18 cakes
19 sauces
20 cereals

TEST 27

1 bitter
2 hot
3 rich
4 sweet
5 spicy
6 bland
7 sour
8 savoury
9 greasy
10 dry
11 delicious
12 burnt

TEST 28

1 f 2 n 3 g 4 m 5 b 6 c 7 l 8 j
9 k 10 e 11 i 12 a 13 d 14 h

TEST 29

cake tin	13
chopping board	1
colander	8
cooling tray	5
dredger	2
frying pan	6
grater	9
ladle	7
mortar and pestle	4
parsley chopper	15
peeler	10
rolling pin	3
scissors	12
spatula	14
whisk	11

TEST 30
1 continue
2 not to have any left
3 become rotten
4 find something in a book
5 take control
6 look at again
7 learn
8 require
9 become
10 cause an object to fall to the ground
1 break a promise
12 become popular

TEST 31
(A)

verb	noun
1 to consume	consumer/consumption
2 to clean	cleanliness/cleaner
3 to poison	poison/poisoning
4 to infect	infection
5 to disinfect	disinfectant
6 to sanitize	sanitation/sanitizer
7 to store	store/storage

(B)
1 sanitize
2 consume
3 disinfectant
4 cleanliness
5 infection
6 store
7 poisoning

Section 5:
FOOD SERVICE

TEST 32
Appetisers
Chef's Pâtés
French Onion Soup
Prawn and Orange Cocktail
Sweet Corn Chowder

Salads
Herring and Apple Salad
Salad Marguery
Tomato Salad

Entrees
Braised leg of Lamb

Chicken Vichy
Entrecôte Steak
Escalope of Veal
Roast Pheasant en Croûte

Vegetarian dishes
Layered Vegetable Terrine
Okra and Courgettes in Lentil Sauce

Vegetables and Side Dishes
Broccoli with Hollandaise Sauce
Cauliflower with Almonds
Leaf Spinach with Diced Bacon
Potato Croquettes
Roast Potatoes

Desserts
Bavarian Apple Strudel
Cold Chocolate Soufflé
Crème Caramel
Pear Hélène

TEST 33
Across
1 corkscrew
4 service cloth
5 candelabra
6 cheese board
7 brigade
8 tray
10 salver
11 wine cooler
12 jug
13 ashtray
14 tureen
15 creases
16 cruet
19 rack
20 bottle opener
23 finger bowl
24 damask

Down
1 crockery
2 cutlery
3 condiments
7 basket
8 tongs
9 tea strainer
10 sideboard
15 cover
17 trolley
18 nutcrackers
21 egg cup

22 doily
Test 34
1 Family
2 Plate
3 French
4 Silver
5 Russian
6 Gueridon
7 Mixed

TEST 35
1 f 2 c 3 a 4 d 5 b 6 e

TEST 36
butter dish	6
coffee pot	3
cup	11
dessert plate	7
jam dish	1
milk jug	2
saucer	10
small knife	9
small napkin	8
sugar bowl	4
teaspoon	12
toast plate	5

TEST 37
1 Just a moment
2 I'm afraid
3 Please
4 Actually
5 Would you like
6 Would you mind
7 Could you
8 Would you like me
9 There's been a slight misunderstanding
10 May I suggest
11 Shall I

Section 6:
RESPONSIBILITIES

TEST 38
accident report book	8
ambulance	13
bandages	3
cotton wool	4
fire alarm	12
fire bucket	9
fire escape	10
fire notice	7
first aid box	1
plasters	2

smoke detector 6
sprinkler 5
warning sign 11

TEST 39
1 exit
2 drill
3 doors, spread
4 extinguish
5 extinguisher
6 raise
7 lifts
8 smoke
9 Evacuate
10 enter
11 safe
12 brigade

TEST 40
1 i 2 l 3 e 4 f 5 k 6 b 7 d 8 a
9 h 10 g 11 j 12 c

TEST 41
1 authorized
2 protect
3 deterrent
4 suspiciously
5 prevent
6 dishonest
7 invisible
8 observe
9 identification
10 securely
11 trustworthy

TEST 42
1 legislation
2 liable
3 exclude
4 purchaser
5 vendor
6 contract
7 proprietor
8 fine
9 prohibited
10 licence
11 licensee
12 admit
13 trespass
14 sentence
15 negligence
16 prosecute
17 compulsory

TEST 43
1 a 2 a 3 b 4 a 5 c 6 b 7 c 8 b
9 c 10 a 11 a

TEST 44
bedbug 14
chicken 4
cockroach 8
flea 5
fly 9
mosquito 13
moth 10
mouse 3
pigeon 6
rat 12
sparrow 7
spider 2
starling 11
wasp 1

TEST 45
(A)
harbour germs
come into contact with
dispose of waste
transmit diseases
spread infection
keep separate
relieve pain
prevent accidents
contaminate food

(B)
1 contaminate food
2 relieve pain
3 prevent accidents
4 spread infection
5 come into contact with
6 dispose of waste
7 keep separate
8 transmit diseases

Section 7:
MANAGEMENT

TEST 46
Across
1 employee
4 part-time
7 tips
8 overtime
10 satisfaction
12 post
13 experience
15 bonus
16 interview
18 resign
20 seasonal
21 motivate
23 appointment

25 pension
26 applicant

Down
1 employer
2 recruit
3 income tax
5 retire
6 qualifications
7 take on
9 appoint
10 supervise
11 wages
14 promotion
17 on duty
19 staff
22 apply
24 earn

TEST 47
1 housekeeper
2 banqueting manager
3 cashier
4 cellarman
5 house porter
6 head waiter
7 dispense bartender
8 pastry cook
9 personnel manager
10 chef
11 advance reservations clerk
12 receptionist
13 pantry maid
14 waitress
15 enquiry clerk

TEST 48
1 exclusive
2 C.V.
3 fitted out
4 at least
5 seeking
6 established
7 prospects
8 benefits
9 candidates
10 innovative
11 initially
12 competitive pay

TEST 49
Rooms
beautifully decorated
bright
elegant
spacious

tastefully furnished
well appointed

Location
beachside
central
conveniently situated
ideally placed
picturesque setting
well located

Food
appetising
delicious
nourishing
gourmet
home-cooked
mouth watering

Hotel
grand
highly recommended
majestic
popular family
traditional
well run

Atmosphere
cheerful
hospitable
peaceful
romantic
tranquil
welcoming

TEST 50

1 (b) a questionnaire
2 (a) satisfy
3 (c) placing
4 (a) campaign
5 (b) offer
6 (c) tempted
7 (a) image
8 (c) promotional
9 (c) publicity
10 (c) article
11 (a) compete

TEST 51

1 storing
2 applications
3 VDUs
4 keyboard
5 screen
6 codes
7 menu
8 printout

9 backed up, disk
10 interface
11 recalled
12 word-processing
13 optics
14 point of sales
15 terminal
16 bar codes
17 electronic mail
18 fax
19 key card system

Section 8:
FINANCIAL AFFAIRS

TEST 52

bulldog clip	7
calculator	10
desk diary	12
diskette	3
hole punch	5
notepad	4
planner	11
printer ribbon	2
ring binder	9
ruler	14
stapler	1
suspension file	8
trays	13
window envelope	6

TEST 53

1 of
2 about, to
3 on
4 to
5 from
6 for
7 on, out
8 about
9 with
10 about
11 to
12 with
13 on, off
14 with
15 for
16 for

TEST 54

Item: Sherry Type: Amontillado		Unit: 75 cl bottle Price: £2.53		
Date	**Reference**	**In**	Out	**Balance**
1st Oct	JB	24		24
2nd Oct	BP		6	18
4th Oct	JB		3	15
6th Oct	JB	24		39
7th Oct	BP		10	29
8th Oct	JB		8	21
12th Oct	JB	24		45
13th Oct	BP		10	35
Maximum stock: 48 Re-order point: 24 Re-order **quantity**		**Minimum stock**: 8 **Suppliers**: Classic Wine Importers Ltd		

TEST 55

1 requisition
2 order
3 delivery note
4 invoice
5 cash discount
6 trade discount
7 statement
8 credit note
9 reminder

TEST 56

addition	4
average	11
balance	3
bar graph	9
cheque book	14
counterfoil	8
entry	2
line graph	10
multiplication	6
paying-in book	7
percentage	13
pie chart	5
purchase account	1
table	15
total	12

TEST 57

1 double entry
2 debit, credit
3 creditors
4 debtors
5 purchase ledger
6 credit customer accounts
7 posted
8 payroll
9 petty cash book
10 visitors' paid outs
11 cash float

TEST 58

1 l 2 e 3 h 4 f 5 a 6 i 7 j 8 b
9 k 10 m 11 d 12 g 13 c

TEST 59
(A)

Country	People	Language	Currency
Canada	Canadians	English/French	Dollar (CAD)
Germany	Germans	German	Deutsche mark (DEM)
Italy	Italians	Italian	Lire (ITL)
Japan	Japanese	Japanese	Yen (JPY)
Australia	Australians	English	Dollar (AUD)
Russia	Russians	Russian	Rouble (RUR)
Switzerland	Swiss	German/French/ Italian	Franc (CHf)
United Kingdom	British	English	Pound (GBP)
United States of America	Americans	English	Dollar (USD)
Sweden	Swedes	Swedish	Krona (SEK)
France	French	French	Franc (FRF)

(B)

1 Francs
2 Italian
3 German
4 Japanese
5 Krona
6 United States of America/USA
7 Roubles
8 Franc

Word list

The numbers after the entries are the tests in which they appear.

A

abrasive, 21
accident report book, 38
accidents, 45
addition, 56
address (v), 12
admit, 42
advance reservations clerk, 47
allocate, 5
ambulance, 38
American plan, 9
annual, 12
appetizers, 32
appetizing, 49
apple, 24
appliance, 23
applicant, 46
applications, 51
apply, 46
appoint, 46
appointment, 46
armed robber, 40
arrivals, 3
arsonist, 40
article, 50
ashtray, 15, 33
asparagus, 25
at least, 48
attendance, 13
attractions, 10
aubergine, 25
Australia, 59
authorized, 41
availability, 5
average, 56

B

back out of, 30
backed up, 51
bad debts, 58
bake, 28
balance, 54, 56
balance sheet, 58
balcony, 18
banana, 24
bandages, 38
banister, 17
bank notes, 7

banqueting manager, 47
banqueting room, 18
bar graph, 56
bar code, 51
basket, 33
baste, 28
bath, 16
bath mat, 16
bath towel, 16
be out of, 30
beachside, 49
bedbug, 44
beetroot, 25
benefits, 4
beverages, 26
bill, 14
binoculars, 1
bitter, 27
blackcurrants, 24
bland, 27
bleach (n), 21
blind (n), 17
bonus, 46
bookings, 4
bookcase, 17
bottle opener, 33
breach, 43
break-even point, 58
brigade, 33, 39
bright, 4
budget, 58
bulldog clip, 52
burglar, 40
burnt, 2
butter beans, 25
butter dish, 36

C

C.V., 48
cabin, 18
cake tin, 29
cakes, 26
calculate, 6
calculator, 52
campaign, 50
Canadians, 59
cancellation, 5
candelabra, 33

candidates, 48
cap, 1
carrier bag, 1
carrot, 25
cash discount, 55
cash float, 57
catch on, 30
cauliflower, 25
ceiling, 17
cellar, 18
cellarman, 44
central, 49
cereals, 26
chambermaid, 15
chamois, 21
chance bookings, 3
check, 15
check out, 6
cheerful, 49
cheese board, 33
cheeses, 26
chef, 47
cheque book, 56
cherries, 24
chicken, 44
chopping board, 29
classroom, 13
clean (v) 15, 31
clientele, 3
cloakroom, 18
coat hanger, 17
coat stand, 17
cockroach, 44
cocktail bar, 18
code, 51
coffee pot, 36
colander, 29
cold, 15
commission rate, 7
compact, 1
compete, 50
competitive, 48
complaint, 14
comply, 43
compulsory, 42
computer billing, 7
condiments 33
conference, 13